THE PROMPT FACTOR

A collection of creative prompts to draw (pun intended) inspiration from.

You are not limited by the prompts alone, but by your own imagination.

Be sure to share your work on Instagram using the hashtag #thepromptfactor to connect with a like minded community!

Enjoy!

Space Monkey

Skeletal Rocket

Celestial Gem

Evil Marshmallow Squad

Bearded Dragon

Dark Majestic Beauty

Uncontrollable Dinner

Joking Banana

Fractal Strawberry

Ornate Lotus

Clever Girl

Zoning Out

Refreshing Elixir

Tree of Life

Obsession

Angry Pencil

A Bad Day

A Great Day

Deadly Roses

Falling Free

Future Vision

Tired Tires

Good Idea Fairy

Social Justice Wizard

Disco Zombie

www.ingramcontent.com/pod-product-compliance
Lightning Source LLC
Chambersburg PA
CBHW081528240526
45465CB00030B/3280